HOW TO

GROW YOUR NETWORK

FAST AND EASILY

Strategies, Insights, and Real-Life Success Stories for Effective Networking and Professional Growth!

RICHARD YORK

Disclaimer:

The information provided in this book is for general informational purposes only. It does not constitute professional advice, and the author and publisher are not responsible for any actions taken or not taken based on the information provided. Always seek the advice of a qualified professional for your specific situation.

Table of Contents

Introduction

In a world driven by connections and collaborations, the ability to grow and nurture a powerful network is a skill that can transform not just your professional journey but your entire narrative. This guide is a roadmap for those ready to harness the potential of strategic networking. By adopting the principles and techniques shared here, you are poised to unlock doors, amplify opportunities, and carve out a trajectory of success previously unimagined.

The Transformative Power of Networking

Allow me to share a personal story that underscores the remarkable impact of effective networking. Not long ago, I found myself navigating the complexities of the professional world, grappling with the challenge of building a network that transcended superficial connections. Embarking on a mission to redefine my approach, I immersed myself in understanding the dynamics of strategic networking. I honed my elevator pitch, perfected my online presence, and actively sought opportunities to engage with professionals in my field. It wasn't long before the seeds I had planted began to bear fruit.

Through a serendipitous encounter at a networking event, I connected with a mentor whose guidance proved instrumental in navigating the intricacies of my industry. This mentor not only opened doors to valuable opportunities but also introduced me to a network of like-minded individuals who shared insights, resources, and support.

This transformative experience is a testament to the potential that lies within intentional and purposeful networking. By applying the principles outlined in this guide, you too can embark on a journey that reshapes your professional narrative, propelling you toward unparalleled growth and success. The time to unlock the doors to your future is now, and it begins with cultivating a network that is not just extensive but inherently impactful.

Seizing Opportunities Through Networking

As my network continued to expand, I found myself presented with opportunities that were once beyond the scope of my imagination. Through the relationships I had cultivated, I secured partnerships, collaborations, and even discovered hidden job prospects. What began as a quest to grow my professional circle soon evolved into a transformative journey that touched every facet of my career.

One notable instance was when a contact I had made at a conference introduced me to a project that aligned perfectly with my skills and aspirations. The collaboration not only elevated my professional standing but also resulted in a project that garnered industry recognition. This not only boosted my credibility but also broadened the scope of my influence within my field.

Cultivating Meaningful Connections

The essence of successful networking lies not just in the number of connections but in the depth and quality of those relationships. By consistently adding value to my network, whether through sharing insights, providing assistance, or simply being a reliable collaborator, I cultivated a network that went beyond transactional exchanges. These meaningful connections not only contributed to my professional growth but also served as a support system during challenging times. Whether seeking advice on navigating career crossroads or celebrating milestones, my network became a source of inspiration, guidance, and encouragement.

A Transformative Journey

In retrospect, the journey of growing my network has been nothing short of transformative. The relationships forged, lessons learned, and opportunities seized have collectively shaped a narrative that transcends traditional career trajectories. Networking, when approached with intention and authenticity, has the power to reshape not just professional outcomes but the very essence of one's story.

As you delve into the strategies outlined in this guide, envision the possibilities that await you. Your network has the potential to be more than a collection of contacts; it can be a dynamic force propelling you towards your goals. Embrace the power of intentional networking, and witness the positive changes it brings to your professional journey. The narrative of success you craft begins with the connections you cultivate today.

1. *Unlocking Networking Success*

Networking is the key that unlocks the doors to opportunities, collaborations, and personal growth. It is a dynamic process that goes beyond mere introductions and business card exchanges; it is about forging genuine connections that resonate on both a professional and personal level. In this section, we will delve into the principles and practices that will empower you to unlock the full potential of networking, drawing insights from real-life experiences, including my own transformative journey.

- **Crafting an Authentic Personal Brand**

The first step to unlocking networking success is cultivating an authentic personal brand. Your brand is not just a professional façade but a reflection of your values, expertise, and unique contributions. Through introspection and refinement, I discovered the power of aligning my personal brand with my aspirations. This clarity not only facilitated more meaningful interactions but also attracted opportunities that resonated with my authentic self.

- **Navigating Networking Events with Purpose**

Attending networking events can be daunting, but with a strategic approach, they become invaluable opportunities for connection. I learned to navigate these settings with purpose, focusing on quality interactions over quantity. By identifying target individuals and engaging in meaningful conversations, I transformed these events into catalysts for growth.

- **Turning Rejections into Opportunities**

Networking success is not immune to setbacks, and rejection is an inevitable part of the journey. Yet, it is in these moments that true resilience is forged. I experienced rejection as a stepping stone rather than a roadblock, using each setback as an opportunity for reflection and improvement. This mindset shift not only strengthened my resolve but also opened unexpected doors.

- **The Power of Reciprocity**

One of the most profound lessons learned on my networking odyssey is the importance of reciprocity. By actively seeking ways to contribute to my network – whether through sharing knowledge, providing support, or facilitating connections – I created a network that thrived on mutual benefit. This approach not only enhanced the depth of my relationships but also positioned me as a valuable asset within my professional community.

- **Adapting in the Digital Landscape**

The digital era has redefined the landscape of networking, presenting both challenges and opportunities. Embracing online platforms with intentionality, I harnessed the power of social media and professional networks to expand my reach. Leveraging technology, I transformed virtual connections into meaningful relationships, demonstrating that the principles of authentic networking transcend physical boundaries.

Unlocking networking success is an ongoing process fueled by continuous learning, adaptability, and a genuine commitment to building meaningful connections. By incorporating these principles into your networking strategy, you too can open doors to a world of possibilities, fostering a network that not only propels your professional endeavours but also enriches the tapestry of your personal and career narrative.

The Power of Purposeful Connections

Depth often surpasses breadth, and purposeful connections stand as the cornerstone of transformative professional relationships. Purposeful connections are not just chance encounters but intentional collaborations that go beyond superficial interactions. I've witnessed first-hand the extraordinary impact of forging connections with a clear purpose.

- **Strategic Alignment**

Purposeful connections are rooted in strategic alignment, where shared goals and values form the foundation of collaboration. By identifying individuals who resonate with your mission and vision, you create a network that becomes a collective force, propelling everyone involved towards shared objectives.

- **Mutual Growth**

The beauty of purposeful connections lies in the reciprocity of growth. Each member of the network contributes unique perspectives, expertise, and resources, fostering an environment where everyone has the opportunity to learn, evolve, and succeed together. Through purposeful connections, I've experienced a collective elevation that transcends individual achievements.

- **Navigating Challenges**

Purposeful connections act as a support system during challenges. Whether facing professional hurdles or seeking guidance, a network founded on purpose becomes a source of strength. In my own journey, these connections provided insights, advice, and sometimes just a reassuring presence during moments of uncertainty.

- **Sustainable Impact**

Unlike fleeting connections, purposeful connections have a lasting impact. They withstand the test of time, evolving and adapting to the changing dynamics of careers and industries. Through purposeful connections, I've built enduring relationships that continue to contribute to my growth and success, reinforcing the notion that true power lies in sustained impact.

The power of purposeful connections lies not just in their existence but in the profound influence they wield on your professional journey. By approaching networking with intentionality, seeking meaningful collaborations, and nurturing purposeful connections, you can tap into a reservoir of collective strength and accelerate your path to success.

2. Building a Strong Foundation

At the heart of successful networking lies a strong foundation, a deliberate groundwork that defines your trajectory. This foundation involves clarifying your networking goals, understanding your unique value proposition, and crafting a compelling personal brand. Through intentional self-reflection and refinement, you pave the way for meaningful connections and set the stage for a network that aligns seamlessly with your aspirations. Building a strong foundation is the catalyst for a purposeful and impactful networking journey.

- **Crafting an Impressive Online Presence**

In the digital age, your online presence is often the first impression you make on the professional world. Crafting an impressive online presence is not just about showcasing your achievements but curating a narrative that resonates with your audience. In this section, we'll explore strategies for building a compelling digital persona, drawing insights from my own experiences in navigating the virtual landscape.

- **Optimizing Your Professional Profiles**

A robust online presence begins with well-optimized professional profiles. Whether on LinkedIn, industry-specific platforms, or personal websites, I discovered the importance of presenting a cohesive and polished image. Through careful attention to detail, such as a compelling bio, professional headshots, and a succinct summary of accomplishments, I transformed my profiles into engaging reflections of my professional journey.

- **Showcasing Your Expertise**

To stand out in the digital crowd, it's essential to showcase your expertise authentically. Regularly sharing insights, articles, or projects related to your field not only positions you as a thought leader but also adds depth to your online presence. In my experience, this consistent sharing not only garnered attention but also initiated valuable conversations and collaborations with like-minded professionals.

- **Engaging in Meaningful Conversations**

An impressive online presence isn't just about self-promotion; it's about engaging in meaningful conversations within your industry. By actively participating in discussions, offering insights, and supporting peers, I found that I not only expanded my network but also enhanced the credibility of my online persona. Authentic engagement fosters connections that go beyond superficial digital interactions.

- **Creating Valuable Content**

Taking the extra step to create and share valuable content amplifies your online presence. Whether through blog posts, videos, or podcasts, I realized that creating content allowed me to showcase my expertise, connect with a broader audience, and leave a lasting impact. This proactive approach not only established me as a go-to resource but also contributed to the overall narrative of my professional brand.

- **Managing Online Reputation**

In the vast digital landscape, reputation management is paramount. I learned to navigate online feedback and criticism gracefully, using it as an opportunity for growth rather than a setback. Actively addressing concerns and fostering open communication showcased my commitment to professionalism and transparency, further solidifying my online reputation.

Crafting an impressive online presence is an ongoing process that requires intention, consistency, and authenticity. By implementing these strategies and drawing from personal experiences, you can transform your digital footprint into a powerful tool that not only attracts opportunities but also aligns seamlessly with your professional narrative.

3. Mastering the Art of Networking Events

Navigating networking events is an art that goes beyond exchanging business cards. It's about strategic engagement, genuine connections, and leaving a lasting impression. From thoughtful preparation to adept conversation skills, mastering the art involves being purposeful, approachable, and memorable. By understanding the nuances of these events, you transform them into opportunities to forge meaningful professional connections that extend beyond the initial handshake.

Navigating Conferences, Mixers, and Meetups

Networking events, whether conferences, mixers, or meetups, are invaluable opportunities to expand your professional circle and cultivate meaningful connections. Navigating these gatherings with finesse requires a strategic approach that goes beyond casual interactions. Drawing from personal experiences, I've discovered key strategies that can elevate your networking game in these dynamic settings.

- **Strategic Pre-Event Planning**

Before attending any event, preparation is key. Research speakers, attendees, and topics of discussion to identify individuals or groups aligned with your objectives. Having a clear agenda ensures that your time is optimized, allowing you to focus on building connections that matter.

- **The Art of Approach**

Approaching new contacts can be daunting, but genuine interest and a well-crafted introduction can break the ice. I've found that initiating conversations with open-ended questions fosters engagement, creating a platform for meaningful dialogue. Confidence, paired with authentic curiosity, forms the foundation for forging connections.

- **Active Listening and Engagement**

In the midst of bustling events, the ability to actively listen sets you apart. Paying attention to others' insights, sharing experiences, and finding common ground are essential. My own experiences have shown that genuine engagement builds rapport, transforming initial encounters into lasting connections.

- **Quality Over Quantity**

While it may be tempting to collect as many business cards as possible, focusing on quality interactions is more fruitful. I learned to prioritize meaningful conversations over superficial exchanges, ensuring that each connection aligns with my professional goals and values.

- **Follow-Up with Intent**

Post-event follow-up is a critical step that many overlook. Send personalized messages expressing gratitude and referencing specific points from your conversation. This not only reinforces the connection but sets the stage for potential collaborations.

During a national industry conference, I applied these strategies and identified a keynote speaker whose work deeply resonated with my interests. By initiating a conversation and expressing genuine appreciation for their insights, I not only gained valuable knowledge but also established a connection that led to a subsequent collaboration on a shared project. This real-life experience underscores the impact of strategic networking in unlocking unforeseen opportunities.

By incorporating these strategies into your approach, you can navigate conferences, mixers, and meetups with purpose, transforming these events into catalysts for meaningful connections and professional growth.

4. Strategic Relationship Building

Strategic relationship building is an intentional process that goes beyond casual connections. It involves identifying key individuals aligned with your goals, offering value, and cultivating genuine partnerships. By understanding the mutual benefits and consistently nurturing these connections, you create a network that strategically propels your professional growth and success.

Targeting Key Connections for Mutual Growth

Successful networking transcends quantity, emphasizing the strategic pursuit of key connections that foster mutual growth. This approach involves identifying individuals whose goals align with yours, forging collaborations that extend beyond mere transactional exchanges. Drawing from my experiences, I've found that targeting key connections is not just about expanding your network but creating a collective force that propels everyone involved towards shared success.

- **Strategic Alignment**

Identifying key connections begins with clarity about your own goals and values. Through intentional self-reflection, I pinpointed areas where my aspirations aligned with those of potential collaborators. This strategic alignment serves as the foundation for cultivating connections that go beyond surface-level interactions.

- **Value Proposition Communication**

Effectively communicating your value proposition is essential when targeting key connections. I learned to articulate what I bring to the table succinctly, emphasizing how collaboration can be mutually beneficial. This transparent communication establishes a solid foundation for meaningful partnerships.

- **Collaborative Projects**

One powerful way to target key connections is by engaging in collaborative projects. By actively seeking opportunities to work together, I've not only deepened relationships but also witnessed accelerated growth. These projects become platforms for shared innovation, learning, and the collective achievement of goals.

- **Shared Learning Experiences**

In my networking journey, I discovered the significance of shared learning experiences. Engaging in professional development or educational initiatives with key connections creates a bond founded on continuous growth. These experiences not only strengthen relationships but also provide a platform for the exchange of insights and knowledge.

A specific instance that highlights the effectiveness of targeting key connections occurred when I identified a professional in my industry whose expertise complemented mine. Through purposeful engagement, we collaboratively organized a workshop that addressed industry challenges. This initiative not only enhanced our individual reputations but also created a shared success story that resonated within our professional community.

- **Reciprocal Support**

Another key aspect of targeting key connections is the establishment of reciprocal support systems. By actively supporting the growth and success of your connections, you foster an environment where everyone is invested in each other's achievements. This reciprocal support amplifies the impact of your network, creating a dynamic ecosystem of mutual growth.

By adopting a strategic mindset and targeting key connections for mutual growth, you elevate your networking efforts from transactional to transformational. This intentional approach not only amplifies individual success but contributes to a collective narrative of achievement and advancement within your professional community.

5. Leveraging Social Media for Impactful Networking

In the digital age, social media has become a powerful tool for forging connections, expanding influence, and creating opportunities. Leveraging social media for impactful networking involves more than just a presence; it requires a strategic approach that aligns with your professional goals. Drawing from personal experiences, I've discovered key strategies to harness the full potential of social platforms in cultivating a robust and influential network.

- **Strategic Platform Selection**

Not all social media platforms are created equal, and each caters to different professional landscapes. I've found that identifying the platforms most relevant to my industry and target audience enhances the efficiency and impact of my networking efforts. Whether it's LinkedIn for professional connections or Twitter for industry insights, strategic platform selection is paramount.

- **Optimizing Profiles for Impact**

Your social media profiles serve as your digital business card. By optimizing them with a professional bio, a high-quality profile picture, and a clear representation of your expertise, you create a compelling online presence. This not only attracts the right connections but also establishes credibility within your industry.

- **Content Sharing and Thought Leadership**

Actively sharing relevant content positions, you as a thought leader in your field. Through consistent sharing of insights, articles, and industry trends, I've been able to initiate meaningful conversations, attract like-minded professionals, and contribute to the broader discourse within my industry. This establishes your presence as a valuable resource and cultivates a network that values your expertise.

- **Engaging Authentically**

Authentic engagement is the cornerstone of impactful networking on social media. I've discovered that responding to comments, participating in discussions, and acknowledging the achievements of others fosters a genuine and supportive community. Authentic engagement not only strengthens existing connections but also attracts new ones who resonate with your approach.

- **Networking Through Groups and Communities**

Joining and actively participating in industry-specific groups or communities amplifies your networking reach. I've found that these spaces provide opportunities for direct interaction with professionals who share common interests. Engaging in discussions, seeking advice, and sharing your own experiences within these groups can lead to valuable connections and collaborations.

A significant illustration of the power of leveraging social media occurred when I actively participated in a Twitter chat related to my industry. Engaging with industry experts, sharing insights, and expressing genuine curiosity resulted in new connections and opportunities. This real-life example emphasizes the impact of proactive social media engagement on expanding one's network.

By incorporating these strategies into your social media approach, you can transform these platforms into dynamic tools for impactful networking. Whether building connections, establishing thought leadership, or fostering collaborative opportunities, social media becomes a conduit for professional growth and influence in the digital landscape.

6. Effective Communication Techniques

In the realm of networking and professional interactions, mastering effective communication is the linchpin for building lasting connections. Here, we explore key techniques that go beyond mere conversation, fostering understanding, collaboration, and a positive professional image.

1. Active Listening

Active listening is the cornerstone of effective communication. By fully engaging in the conversation, showing genuine interest, and responding thoughtfully, you not only absorb valuable information but also convey respect and attentiveness. This simple yet powerful technique establishes a foundation for meaningful connections.

2. Clear and Concise Messaging

Communicate your ideas with clarity and conciseness. Crafting a message that is straightforward and to the point ensures that your audience grasps the essential information. I've learned that clarity in communication enhances understanding, making interactions more impactful.

3. Non-Verbal Communication

Non-verbal cues, such as body language and facial expressions, play a significant role in conveying your message. Maintaining eye contact, using open body language, and being mindful of your expressions contribute to a positive and approachable image. These non-verbal elements complement your words and enhance the overall effectiveness of your communication.

4. Tailoring Communication Style

Adapt your communication style to the preferences and expectations of your audience. Whether it's adjusting the level of formality or using industry-specific language, tailoring your approach ensures that your message resonates with those you are communicating with. Flexibility in communication style allows you to connect with a diverse range of individuals.

5. Constructive Feedback

Providing and receiving feedback is an integral part of professional growth. When delivering feedback, focus on specific behaviours, be constructive, and offer actionable suggestions for improvement. Likewise, being open to receiving feedback demonstrates a commitment to continuous improvement and strengthens professional relationships.

6. Empathy and Emotional Intelligence

Understanding the emotions of others and expressing empathy builds a strong foundation for effective communication. Acknowledge perspectives, validate feelings, and be attuned to the emotional context of a conversation. This fosters a sense of connection and mutual understanding.

7. Confidence and Positivity

Confidence in communication is empowering, but it should be balanced with humility. Projecting a positive attitude, even in challenging situations, contributes to a constructive and collaborative atmosphere. Confidence, when paired with humility, creates a compelling and approachable professional demeanour.

8. Art of Persuasion

Mastering the art of persuasion involves presenting your ideas convincingly. Back your arguments with facts, use compelling storytelling, and highlight the benefits. Effective persuasion is not about manipulation but about presenting a compelling case that resonates with your audience.

In a professional setting, I encountered a situation where clear and concise communication was essential to align team members on a critical project. By employing active listening, tailoring my communication style to the diverse team members, and providing constructive feedback, we successfully navigated challenges and achieved project milestones.

Elevator Pitches and Conversational Mastery

Crafting a compelling elevator pitch is an art in concise storytelling. Mastering conversations involves active listening, authentic engagement, and adapting to various communication styles. These skills are the keys to leaving a lasting impression in brief encounters. Elevator pitches and conversational mastery are not just tools; they're the gateways to sparking interest, making memorable connections, and opening doors to new possibilities in your professional journey.

7. Giving and Receiving: The Art of Networking Reciprocity

Networking is not a one-way street; it thrives on the principles of reciprocity— the exchange of value between individuals. Mastering the art of giving and receiving within your professional network creates a dynamic ecosystem of support, collaboration, and mutual growth. Here, we delve into the principles that underpin this art, drawing from real-life experiences that underscore the transformative impact of reciprocal networking.

1. Proactive Giving

Sharing Insights and Resources: Actively contribute to your network by sharing valuable insights, industry trends, or relevant resources. Whether through online platforms, articles, or in-person discussions, proactive giving establishes your credibility and positions you as a valuable resource within your professional community.

Offering Support and Assistance: Extend a helping hand to your network by offering support or assistance when needed. Whether it's providing advice, making introductions, or offering your skills, proactive giving strengthens relationships and fosters a culture of reciprocity.

2. Strategic Receiving

Being Open to Opportunities: Embrace opportunities that come your way. Whether it's a chance to collaborate on a project, attend a networking event, or take on a new challenge, being open to opportunities positions you to receive the benefits of reciprocal networking.

Receptive to Feedback: Actively seek and be receptive to feedback. Constructive feedback is a valuable gift that contributes to your professional growth. By embracing feedback, you demonstrate a commitment to improvement and create an environment where others feel comfortable sharing insights.

3. **Building Meaningful Connections**

Fostering Relationships, Not Transactions: Prioritize building meaningful, long-lasting relationships over transactional exchanges. Genuine connections are the foundation of successful reciprocal networking. Take the time to understand the goals, challenges, and aspirations of your connections, and actively contribute to their success.

Recognizing and Acknowledging Contributions: Acknowledge and appreciate the contributions of others within your network. Whether it's publicly recognizing achievements, expressing gratitude, or simply acknowledging the efforts of your peers, these gestures strengthen the bonds of reciprocity.

A notable example from my networking journey involved a collaborative project with a connection in a complementary field. By combining our expertise, resources, and networks, we not only achieved success in the project but also created a mutually beneficial collaboration that extended beyond the initial venture.

4. Sustainable Reciprocity

Long-Term Relationship Building: Reciprocal networking is a long-term investment. Focus on building sustained relationships rather than seeking immediate returns. Consistent giving and receiving over time create a network that evolves and grows collectively.

Adaptability in Reciprocity: Be adaptable in your approach to reciprocity. The needs and dynamics of your network may change over time, and being flexible in how you contribute and receive ensures the ongoing effectiveness of your networking efforts.

Mastering the art of networking reciprocity transforms your professional connections from transactional to transformative. By embracing the principles of proactive giving and strategic receiving, you contribute to a thriving network where mutual support and growth become the norm. In the tapestry of professional relationships, the art of giving and receiving weaves a narrative of collaborative success and shared accomplishments.

Creating Win-Win Relationships

Successful networking is not a zero-sum game; it thrives on mutual benefit. Cultivating win-win relationships involves understanding others' needs, aligning goals, and actively contributing value. By fostering collaborations where both parties thrive, you build a network grounded in reciprocity. The art lies in creating synergies where everyone involved not only achieves individual success but also contributes to the collective advancement of the network.

8. Overcoming Networking Challenges

Networking, while essential for professional growth, often presents challenges that require resilience and strategic navigation. Addressing these obstacles head-on is crucial for building a robust professional network. Here, we explore common networking challenges and effective strategies to overcome them.

1. Networking Anxiety and Shyness

Strategy: Start small and gradually expand your comfort zone. Begin with smaller networking events, engage in one-on-one conversations, and practice active listening. Set realistic goals for each interaction to build confidence over time.

2. Fear of Rejection

Strategy: Reframe rejection as a natural part of the networking process. Instead of viewing it as a personal failure, consider it an opportunity to learn and refine your approach. Understand that not every interaction will lead to a connection, and that's perfectly normal.

3. Balancing Quantity and Quality

Strategy: Prioritize quality over quantity in your networking efforts. Building meaningful connections takes time and genuine engagement. Focus on fostering a few deep relationships rather than spreading yourself too thin across numerous superficial connections.

4. Navigating Online Networking

Strategy: Leverage the digital landscape strategically. Create a compelling online presence, actively participate in relevant groups or forums, and initiate conversations with thought leaders in your field. Balance online interactions with in-person networking to maximize your reach.

5. Time Constraints

Strategy: Efficiently manage your time by setting clear networking goals and priorities. Attend events that align with your objectives, and use technology to streamline online interactions. Make the most of brief encounters by having a concise elevator pitch ready.

6. Lack of Confidence in Self-Promotion

Strategy: Focus on promoting your value rather than yourself. Share success stories, highlight your skills, and discuss the value you bring to collaborations. Authentic self-promotion is about showcasing your expertise and how it aligns with the needs of your network.

7. Maintaining Follow-Up Momentum

Strategy: Develop a systematic follow-up process. Immediately connect with new contacts on professional platforms, send personalized follow-up emails, and schedule periodic check-ins. Consistent, thoughtful follow-up reinforces your commitment to building lasting connections.

8. Networking Fatigue

Strategy: Recognize when to recharge. Networking fatigue is normal, and taking breaks to recharge allows you to bring fresh energy to your interactions. Prioritize self-care, set realistic expectations, and celebrate small wins to stay motivated.

9. Diversity and Inclusivity Challenges

Strategy: Actively seek out diverse networking opportunities and engage with individuals from different backgrounds. Attend events that promote inclusivity, and be intentional about expanding your network beyond familiar circles. Embrace diversity as a strength in your professional connections.

10. Fear of Being Perceived as Opportunistic

Strategy: Approach networking with authenticity and genuine interest. Focus on building relationships rather than immediately seeking opportunities. When your interactions are rooted in authenticity, you'll naturally avoid the perception of opportunism.

A personal experience involved overcoming networking anxiety by attending smaller industry gatherings. Through consistent practice, I transformed my anxiety into a strength. Engaging in more intimate settings allowed me to build deeper connections, ultimately boosting my confidence in larger networking events.

Overcoming networking challenges is an ongoing journey that requires adaptability and perseverance. By addressing these obstacles with strategic approaches and learning from real-life experiences, you can navigate the networking landscape with confidence, resilience, and a focus on building meaningful professional connections.

Turning Obstacles into Opportunities

In the landscape of professional growth, obstacles are not roadblocks but stepping stones. Each challenge presents a unique opportunity for learning, adaptation, and innovation. The art lies in reframing setbacks, leveraging adversity for personal and career development, and discovering unforeseen possibilities. By embracing challenges as catalysts for growth, you transform obstacles into avenues leading to new opportunities and enhanced resilience on your professional journey.

9. Sustaining and Expanding Your Network

Building a professional network is not a one-time endeavour but an ongoing process that requires both nurturing existing connections and actively seeking new opportunities. Here, we explore strategies for sustaining and expanding your network, ensuring its continuous growth and relevance in your professional journey.

1. Consistent Engagement

Sustaining: Regularly engage with your existing network by participating in industry events, online discussions, and sharing relevant content. Consistency in engagement demonstrates your ongoing commitment to the relationship.

Expanding: Actively seek new opportunities for engagement, such as attending diverse events, joining new professional groups, and contributing to discussions in emerging forums. This proactivity introduces you to a broader spectrum of professionals and industries.

2. Strategic Follow-Up

Sustaining: Implement a strategic follow-up routine with existing connections. Schedule periodic check-ins, offer support, and celebrate their achievements. Thoughtful follow-up reinforces the depth of your relationships.

Expanding: Extend your follow-up approach to new connections. After initial interactions, promptly connect on professional platforms, express gratitude, and initiate future collaboration discussions. Timely follow-up establishes a foundation for continued engagement.

3. Leveraging Technology

Sustaining: Utilize technology to stay connected. Leverage professional networking platforms, maintain an updated online presence, and use tools for efficient communication. Technology streamlines sustained connections.

Expanding: Explore emerging platforms and technologies that align with your industry. Stay abreast of innovations that can enhance your networking efforts and provide new avenues for expansion.

4. Offering Value

Sustaining: Continually find ways to add value to your existing network. Share insights, offer assistance, and contribute to discussions. Being a valuable resource strengthens your position within the network.

Expanding: Extend your value proposition to new connections. Identify how your expertise or resources can benefit others. Offering value establishes credibility and fosters meaningful connections.

5. Strategic Networking Events:

Sustaining: Attend industry-specific events where your existing connections are likely to be present. This reinforces your presence within the network and provides opportunities for face-to-face interactions. - *Expanding:* Seek out new networking events that align with your evolving goals. Diversify your attendance to include events in adjacent industries or interdisciplinary forums, broadening the scope of your network.

6. Intentional Relationship Building

Sustaining: Be intentional about nurturing relationships. Listen actively, offer support during challenging times, and celebrate successes together. Authenticity in relationship building contributes to sustained connections.

Expanding: Approach new connections with the same level of intentionality. Invest time in getting to know individuals, understanding their goals, and identifying ways in which you can contribute to each other's success.

7. Mentorship and Guidance

Sustaining: Cultivate mentorship relationships within your existing network. Seek guidance from seasoned professionals, and offer mentorship to those in earlier stages of their careers. Mentorship adds depth to your network.

Expanding: Actively seek out new mentorship opportunities. Identify individuals whose experiences align with your goals, and express genuine interest in learning from their insights. Mentorship expands both your knowledge and your network.

Regularly engaging with a mentor from my existing network allowed me to receive ongoing guidance and insights. Our consistent communication not only sustained the relationship but also led to collaborative projects. Actively participating in a cross-industry conference introduced me to professionals from diverse fields. By leveraging the shared experiences and expertise of these new connections, I expanded both the depth and breadth of my network.

Sustaining and expanding your network is a dynamic balance between nurturing existing relationships and seeking new opportunities. By adopting a proactive and strategic approach, you ensure that your network remains a vibrant and influential asset throughout your professional journey.

Cultivating Long-Term Professional Relationships

Building enduring professional connections transcends mere transactions. It's a deliberate and ongoing investment. The key is in consistent engagement, genuine care, and mutual support. By actively nurturing relationships over time, you foster a network that becomes a reliable source of insights, opportunities, and collaborative ventures. The art lies not just in making connections but in sustaining a tapestry of relationships that stand the test of time, contributing to your growth and success throughout your professional journey.

10. Networking for Career Advancement

In the contemporary professional landscape, networking is not just a valuable skill; it's a catalyst for career advancement. Purposeful and strategic networking can open doors to new opportunities, provide valuable insights, and significantly contribute to your overall professional growth. Below are how to leverage networking for career advancement:

1. Clarify Career Goals

Strategy: Before diving into networking, have a clear understanding of your career goals. Define the skills you want to develop, the roles you aspire to, and the industries you are interested in. This clarity forms the foundation for strategic networking.

2. Build a Strong Online Presence

Strategy: Optimize your professional profiles on platforms like LinkedIn. Showcase your achievements, skills, and aspirations. Regularly share industry insights and engage in relevant discussions. A robust online presence attracts opportunities and connections.

3. Identify Key Influencers

Strategy: Identify and connect with key influencers in your industry. These could be thought leaders, successful professionals, or individuals holding influential positions. Engaging with influencers provides access to valuable insights and expands your network's reach.

4. Attend Industry-Specific Events

Strategy: Actively participate in conferences, seminars, and networking events within your industry. These gatherings provide opportunities to meet professionals, learn about industry trends, and make connections that can contribute to your career advancement.

5. Seek Mentorship

Strategy: Establish mentor-mentee relationships with individuals who have advanced in their careers. A mentor can provide guidance, share experiences, and offer valuable advice that accelerates your professional development.

6. Join Professional Associations

Strategy: Become a member of professional associations related to your field. Attend their events, engage in discussions, and volunteer for leadership roles. Being an active member enhances your visibility and credibility within the professional community.

7. Strategic Informational Interviews

Strategy: Conduct informational interviews with professionals who have achieved career success in your desired field. Gain insights into their career paths, seek advice, and use these connections to broaden your understanding of industry dynamics.

8. Collaborate on Projects

Strategy: Actively seek collaborative projects or initiatives within your network. Contributing to projects not only enhances your skills but also exposes you to different facets of your industry. Successful collaborations can lead to career-advancing opportunities.

9. Continuous Learning

Strategy: Attend workshops, webinars, and training sessions relevant to your field. Networking within educational contexts introduces you to both industry experts and peers who share similar learning goals.

Attending an industry conference allowed me to connect with a senior executive in my field. Engaging in thoughtful conversations, I expressed my career aspirations. This connection eventually led to mentorship, valuable insights, and eventually, a career advancement opportunity within their organization.

10. Strategic Job Searching

Strategy: Leverage your network during job searches. Seek referrals from connections within the companies you are interested in. Personal connections can often open doors and provide insights that are not available through traditional job applications.

11. Stay Authentic and Grateful

Strategy: Be authentic in your interactions. Express gratitude for advice, support, and opportunities. Authenticity builds trust, and gratefulness strengthens the bonds within your network.

Leveraging networking for career advancement requires a combination of strategic planning, genuine interactions, and continuous learning. By actively cultivating a network aligned with your career goals, you position yourself for opportunities that can propel your professional journey forward.

Turning Connections into Opportunities

In the realm of networking, the true alchemy lies in transforming connections into tangible opportunities.

It's not just about who you know but how you strategically leverage those relationships. This process involves active engagement, showcasing your value, and being attuned to possibilities. By cultivating genuine connections and consistently demonstrating your expertise, you unlock the potential for collaborations, career advancements, and unforeseen prospects. The art lies in recognizing the openings, creating synergies, and turning each connection into a stepping stone toward your professional aspirations.

Conclusion

In the journey of crafting this guide on networking, we've explored the intricate web of professional connections, dissecting strategies, and sharing real-life experiences to empower you to unlock the full potential of your network. As we draw to a close, consider this conclusion a catalyst for your continued growth in the realm of networking.

Networking is not just a collection of contacts but a dynamic force that shapes your professional narrative. From the initial steps of building a strong foundation to the nuances of sustaining and expanding your network, you've gained insights into the art and science of fostering meaningful connections. The strategies shared are not mere prescriptions but tools for you to wield, adapt, and personalize on your unique journey.

As you navigate the intricacies of networking, remember the power of reciprocity, the impact of purposeful connections, and the transformative potential of giving and receiving. Seize opportunities to strategically engage both online and offline, recognizing that your digital presence is as crucial as your in-person interactions.

Reflect on the challenges you may encounter, acknowledging that resilience and adaptability are key to overcoming them. Embrace networking not as a transaction but as a lifelong process that evolves with your career, industry, and aspirations. The stories shared serve as beacons, illustrating that every setback can be a stepping stone, and every connection a door to unforeseen opportunities.

In conclusion, your professional network is not just a means to an end; it is a living, breathing ecosystem that reflects your journey, ambitions, and the collective narrative of those you connect with. Approach networking with intentionality, authenticity, and a commitment to continuous learning.

As you step forward into the vast landscape of your professional future, may your network be a source of inspiration, support, and boundless possibilities. Remember, the art of networking is not just about who you know but how you leverage those connections to shape a narrative of success, impact, and fulfilment in your career. Your network is not a static entity; it is a dynamic force that has the potential to propel you to new heights and redefine what is possible. Unlock the doors, forge the connections, and let your professional network be a beacon guiding you towards the extraordinary. Your story is waiting to be written, and your network is the canvas on which it unfolds. Here's to the journey ahead and the boundless opportunities that networking brings.